Mulled wine and mistletoe; mince pies
and cakes; crackers and decorations;
everything you need to know for a
truly delicious and traditional
festive celebration.

GOLDENHAIR & CURLYHEAD

Merry Christmas

ETIQUETTE
FOR A
TRADITIONAL
CHRISTMAS

Copper Beech Publishing

Published in Great Britain by
Copper Beech Publishing Ltd
© Jan Barnes 2000

ISBN
978 1 898617 27 3
1 898617 27 9
A CIP catalogue record for this book is available from
The British Library
Victorian scraps cover design supplied by Beryl Peters.
Tom Smith crackers are now distributed by
Napier Industries. 'The parcel department at Messrs Tom
Smith & Co, 1891' and 'Motor Cycle Crackers' reproduced
with their kind permission.
Party games reproduced from 'How to Entertain Your
Guests' published by Copper Beech Publishing.

Copper Beech Publishing Ltd
P O Box 159 East Grinstead
Sussex England RH19 4FS

This old English Carol really depicts the Nativity scene:

"As Joseph was a-walking
He heard an angel sing:
This night shall be the birthtime
of Christ the Heav'nly King.

He neither shall be born
In house nor in hall
Nor in the place of Paradise,
But in an ox's stall.

He neither shall be clothed
In purple nor in pall,
But in fair white linen
That usen babies all.

He neither shall be rocked
In silver nor in gold,
But in a wooden manger,
That resteth on the mould.

As Joseph was a-walking
There did an angel sing,
And Mary's child at midnight
Was born to be our King.

Then be ye glad, good people,
This night of all the year
And light ye up your candles,
For His star it shineth clear."

*The traditional Christmas we celebrate today is
mostly based on the Christmas celebrations
in Victorian England.
Queen Victoria's nursery was growing all the time,
and the centre of Christmas life then, as now, was
the children. Familiar images of the season, such as
the glittering Christmas tree, were introduced
by her husband, Prince Albert.
However, other parts of today's celebrations, such
as the bringing in of evergreens, have their origins
many thousands of years before.
The celebration of the midwinter solstice evolved
into the Christmas we know today.*

A ROYAL CHRISTMAS

In 1904, a ladies' magazine detailed a Royal Christmas Day as follows:

"The first sound to greet the guests at Sandringham is that of bagpipes ... the little Princes and Princesses are in a high state of excitement, for has not Santa Claus, in the darkness of night, been distributing his bounty with lavish hands?

The Royal Family keep up Christmas at Sandringham in a right Royal and old-fashioned way. Tasteful decorations with holly and mistletoe abound everywhere.

Everyone comes down to the dining-room where breakfast is taken *en famille*. After breakfast, the Royal Family and guests go on a tour to view the decorations; and then, if the weather is fine, they walk to church.

Then comes luncheon, which is the children's dinner – attended of course, by all members of the family. The Christmas pudding is brought in, blazing up merrily.

Some part of the afternoon is devoted to walking and riding; a tour of the stables and kennels is a great feature! Pets are visited and fed with sugar by Royal hands.

Afternoon tea is an informal meal, partaken of in the Grand Salon, the Queen presiding at the tea-table.

And now comes a very exciting time for the children. The doors of a certain saloon have been kept rigorously fastened ... Her Majesty and other members of her family having duly dressed a large Christmas tree therein. The door is opened and the Royal children evince the greatest delight at the Christmas tree ablaze with lights and weighed down with presents. Afterwards, all sorts of games are entered into with a heartiness and zest that must surely appeal to everyone.

Dinner comes along at 8.45. On the tables there is a brilliant display of glittering plate and glass, and the servants look resplendent in their Royal liveries. Nor are the servants forgotten, for they have a Christmas dinner, though not on the actual day. But when it does take place, it is a right merry gathering."

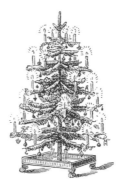

Evergreens have been brought into the house at midwinter since Roman times. They bring good luck and symbolise eternal life.

EVERGREENS

From earliest times, churches and homes were decorated with bay, rosemary, holly, ivy and privet. The addition of the chrysanthemum, satin flowers and other everlastings, mingling with the red berry of the holly and the waxen one of the mystic mistletoe, have a very pleasing and cheerful effect.

> **"With holly and ivy**
> **So green and so gay**
> **We deck up our houses**
> **As fresh as the day:**
> **With bays and rosemary**
> **With laurel compleate,**
> **And every one now**
> **Is a king in conceite."**
> **Christmas song 1695**

TRADITIONAL DECORATIONS

What a happy time can be had in preparing the home for Christmas, and making it look as pretty as possible by the aid of the bright-berried holly and historic mistletoe, besides the lovely winter flowers which help to make the rooms look so charming.

This is a part of the Christmas planning in which every member of the household can lend a helping hand, but it must be superintended by one who possesses the gift of good taste!

The best way to set about the actual decoration is to first of all make up your scheme for the different rooms, and not to leave it all to the last moment, when the decorations are just bundled anyhow behind pictures.

Badly arranged decorations keep tumbling down and annoying everyone, because they are not securely fastened!

Don't forget!

Don't forget to save a nice sprig of holly to stick in the pudding before it is brought to the table, and if the berries are very plentiful, pick out some nice little pieces which will make buttonholes for the boys and pretty hair ornaments for the girls, so that everybody and everything will have a Christmas aspect; and, above all, don't forget the piece of mistletoe underneath the hall lamp.

Pretty ropes of green leaves are easily made with the aid of a carpet needle and some fine twine. Thread the leaves on to the twine as you would when threading beads.

These ropes look very well hanging from the corners of the room and meeting under the chandelier, with a bunch of flowers hanging from the middle, where the four ends meet. The ropes also look very pretty if artificial flowers are entwined with the green leaves.

Decorations should add to the beauty of the home,
and not mar it.

HOLLY, IVY AND MISTLETOE

The first essential will be the purchasing of the holly &c, and the best way to do this is to go round to the shops with one of your sturdy boys or brothers.

Some people are fortunate enough to be able to collect wild holly and evergreens but if you must buy, be sure to find the shop that has the best of the goods you want showing. Get the holly as full of berries as possible, as their bright red colour seems to shed out a ray of warmth and welcome to all.

Holly and Ivy are said to represent man and woman and their struggle for mastery in the house. If prickly holly is brought in first, the man will have mastery. Smooth holly first, gives the wife the upper hand.

*Years ago, mistletoe was thought to have powers of
fertility, which is possibly why we kiss under it.
You have been warned!*

The Christmas block or Yule Log:
"Heap on more wood – the wind is chill
but let it whistle as it will
We'll keep our Christmas merry still"

THE YULE LOG

A massive piece of wood should be selected (frequently the rugged root of a tree), and it should be brought into the great hall or kitchen with much rejoicing and merriment.

It is said that the Yule Log should be of the ash tree because the baby Jesus was first washed and dressed by an ash wood fire made by the shepherds hurriedly because it was the only wood that would burn while still green and not spit.

This Yule Log should burn from Christmas Eve until Twelfth Night when it should be extinguished and a piece of the wood put by for the following year. With this fragment of log, households over the years have felt secure against the assault of hobgoblins.

Save the ashes from the Yule Log and use them to protect the house and cure toothache.

CANDLES

A feature of Mediaeval Christmas Eve was the tall Christmas candles, with their wreaths of evergreens, which were lighted at the same time as the Yule Log and placed on the upper table.

It was thought unlucky to snuff these candles out. Christmas was often called the 'Feast of Lights'.

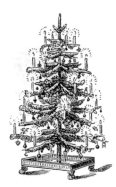

The custom of singing carols around the bedecked and twinkling branches of the tree loaded with gifts is loved by all.

CHRISTMAS STOCKING

The tradition of the Christmas Stocking is said to have begun when St Nicholas, wishing to provide dowries for three poor girls anonymously, threw bags of gold through their window which fell on their stockings hanging by the fire to dry.

The traditional contents of the stocking are not expensive, but symbolic and should include: an apple for health; an orange for a treat; coal for warmth; salt for good luck, and a new penny for wealth in the year to come.

🔔 THE CHRISTMAS TREE 🔔

The Christmas Tree was introduced from the continent into England in the reign of Queen Victoria. Her husband, Prince Albert popularised the fir tree part of the festive celebrations.

Much taste can be displayed (and expense also incurred) in preparing its glittering and attractive fruit.

Choose a tree as large as possible and plant it firmly in a wooden tub. Plenty of golden and silver balls and other ornaments may be obtained from large stores and pieces of cotton wool resting lightly along the tops of the branches give a pretty 'snow-flake' effect. Other novelties, such as Father Christmases, sweets and Bon Bons will add to the excitement.

It is delightful to watch the animated expectation and enjoyment of the children as the treasures are displayed and distributed; their parents equally participating in the pleasure.

SANTA CLAUS

The story of **Santa Claus** or St Nicholas goes back to the beginning of the 4th century. Nicholas, Bishop of Myra on the coast of Lycia was very generous in helping those in distress, but he did so secretly; when the benefactor was discovered, he was canonised and became St Nicholas, and afterwards, any unknown gift was attributed to his kindness.

The familiar look of Santa Claus, or Father Christmas, was created by the Americans, who gave him his red coat, white hair and beard.

The original early Victorian mottoes were mainly love verses ...

**The sweet crimson rose with its beautiful hue
Is not half so deep as my passion for you.**

CHRISTMAS CRACKERS

The **Christmas cracker,** based on the French 'Bon Bon' came to England in the mid 19th century.

It is usually accepted that the confectioner Tom Smith discovered Bon Bons, then just sugared almonds wrapped in tissue paper, on a trip to Paris in 1840 and introduced the idea into England. This simple notion would, over the next seven years, evolve into the cracker.

It is said that Tom Smith got the idea of the snap while sitting by the fire listening to the logs crackling, and created the cracker by adding first the motto, then the snap and finally the novelty and paper hat.

At the turn of the 19th and 20th centuries, the demand for crackers, and especially those which celebrated current trends and events, was high. Now, it would be hard to imagine a Christmas without crackers as part of the festive celebrations.

🧸 INVOLVING THE CHILDREN 🧸

The decorations of the nursery or playroom can be left entirely in the children's own hands.

Supply the children with sheets of pretty coloured tissue paper (which can be bought at two and sometimes three sheets for a penny), some scissors, and a pot of paste.

Let the children cut the paper into strips of about one inch wide, and ten inches long, paste one together so as to form a loop, and then thread the rest each through the other so as they form a chain.

Miniature Trees
Let the children have a miniature version of the tree in their rooms and decorate it themselves!

Candle Lamps

Using a clean jar and paint, draw Father Christmas, a snowman or a tree, dot on the snow effect with white paint and put a night candle in the bottom of the jar.

Orange Pomanders

Years ago, the aroma from these pomanders would disguise unpleasant smells. Push cloves (stalk end first) into the orange. Tie ribbon around the orange and hang on the Christmas tree for decorative effect.

These make very pretty decorations and will keep the children busily employed during those exciting restless evenings just before Christmas, when they don't feel as if they can be amused with their ordinary games and toys.

CARDS AND GIFTS

It is thought that the first Christmas card was probably commissioned by Henry Cole and designed by John Horsley, a member of the Royal Academy.

A thousand cards were printed in 1846, which was considered a large scale. This first card, represented a family of three generations round a table quaffing wine.

It was lithographed and then coloured by hand. Cards did not become common until 1870, the earliest types being simple in design.

The first appeal to 'Post Early for Christmas' was made in 1880.

CHRISTMAS PRESENTS FOR ALL.

Some Seasonable Suggestions.

GRANDFATHER.

Reading Glass.
Book Holder.
Silk Muffler.
Reading Lamp.

GRANDMOTHER.

Spectacle Chatelaine
Dorothy Bag.   [Case.
Dainty Perfume.
Felt Slippers.

FATHER.

Pocket Stamp Case.
Flat Pocket Pencil.
Walking Stick.
Shaving Materials.
Smoking Coat.

MOTHER.

Card Case.
Initial Handkerchiefs.
Umbrella.
Favourite Poets.
Opera Glasses.

SONS.

Shoe-Blacking Case.
Tie Pin.
Watch Chain Charm.
Hanging Clothes Brushes.
Fancy Waistcoat.
Ring.

DAUGHTERS.

Glove and Handkerchief
Stock Ties.   [Case.
Fancy Hair-Combs.
Initial Brush and Comb.
Silk Blouse Length.
Bracelet.

FOR THE CHILDREN.

Money-box.
Waterproof Satchel.
Coloured Crayons.
Clockwork Train.
Music Case.
Muff and Fur.
Handkerchiefs.
Drawing Slate.

Books of Adventure.
Indoor Games.
Toy Soldiers.
Steam Engine.
Tea Set.
Fur-lined Gloves.
Box of Paints.
Dancing Slippers.

FOR THE BABY.

Silver Rattle.
Rag Doll.
Little Woollen Jacket.

Silver " Baby " Brooch.
Sleeve Tie-ups and Sash.
Silk Embroidered Bib.

FOR THE MAID.

Warm Gloves.
Caps.
Handkerchiefs.

Aprons.
House Shoes.
Warm Blouse.

These 'seasonable suggestions' were offered in 1904 in a women's magazine.

31

Charles **Dickens** wrote his famous tale '*A Christmas Carol*' in 1843. This story, with its characters - Bob Cratchit, the conscientious clerk, the unfortunate Tiny Tim, and of course, Scrooge who, through this tale, learns to mend his ways - is familiar to many at Christmas-time. Families gather round to hear father - or grandfather read the cautionary tale; children learn from this yearly reminder that it is their duty to continue kindness and goodwill in the coming year.

"Who can listen to objectors regarding such a book as this? It seems to me a national benefit, and to every man and woman who reads it a personal kindness."
W M Thackeray about 'A Christmas Carol'

FESTIVE FAYRE
AND SOCIAL DRINKS

"Now thrice welcome, Christmas
Which brings us good cheer,
Minc'd pies and plum-porridge,
Good ale and strong beer;
With pig, goose and capon
The best that may be
So well doth the weather
And our stomachs agree."
1695

✢ GOOSE AND TURKEY ✢

During the 19th century, many families had goose for Christmas dinner and saved up for it all year by paying into a 'Goose Club'.

The turkey was not introduced into England until the 16th century from America where it grew wild. It soon superseded other dainties for the festive feast.

Victorian families took their Christmas goose to the local baker to be cooked in his large oven on Christmas morning.

The pudding must be boiled by daybreak on Christmas Day or else two young men must take the maiden (the cook) by the arms and run her round the market place till she is ashamed of her laziness.
Old custom

❧ PLUM PUDDING ❧

Plum pudding at Christmas is found on the menu of rich and poor, along with mince pies.

The making and serving of plum pudding at Christmas is, in fact, quite a ritual. The more it is stirred the better it is – and each member of the family is supposed to come and give a helping hand and a good stir. It has become customary for each person to make a wish as they stir the mixture.

A 'lucky' sixpence is often put inside the pudding – the finding of which is a cause of great excitement and hilarity. The plum pudding is gaily decorated with a sprig of holly, and the traditional way of serving is to pour hot brandy over it, to set it alight and carry it in to the dining-room where all lights are out.

Plum puddings are supposed to improve and 'mature' with keeping, and many people in England actually keep them for a year!

CHRISTMAS PUDDING.

WHEN merry, frosty Christmas comes,
Mamma takes currants, peel, and plums;
Spice, raisins, flour, and eggs she takes,
And with them all a pudding makes;
So we are glad when Christmas comes
And brings us puddings full of plums.

CHRISTMAS (PLUM) PUDDING RECIPE

2oz flour
1 level teaspoon mixed spice
1½ level teaspoon cinnamon
½ level teaspoon nutmeg
4oz mixed candied peel
4oz chopped blanched almonds
1 tablespoon black treacle
4oz fine breadcrumbs
4oz each melted butter and sugar
Grated apple
1 small carrot grated
1lb mixed fruit, preferably:
8oz raisins, 4oz sultanas, 4oz currants
Grated rind and juice of 1 large lemon
2 eggs
¼ pint ale + 2 tablespoons brandy

Mix all ingredients thoroughly. Stir well and leave the
mixture for one day and one night to mature. Press
into large basin and cover with greased paper. Cover
with paste made from six ounces flour and water.
Steam or boil six to eight hours. Remove damp covers
and when cold put on dry paper. Steam a further
two to four hours before serving.

⋇   MINCE PIES   ⋇

Mince pies are probably the descendants of **Roman sweetmeats** given away at the midwinter festival. The well-known minced or Christmas pie is of considerable antiquity. Early writers report them to be made of 'tongues, chicken, eggs, sugar, currants, lemon and orange peel with various spices' although nowadays it is a sweet pie with no meats included.

The cover or case of each pie was traditionally oblong in imitation of the manger where the Saviour was laid.

"Good cheer doth so abound as if all the world were made of mince pies, plum pudding and frumity"
Poor Robin's Almanack 1676

A WELL-TRIED RECIPE FOR MINCE PIES

The following recipe is a well-tried and approved one and has been handed down through generations:

1lb suet, chopped fine
1lb raisins, stoned
1lb currants, cleaned and dry
1lb apples chopped fine
Two or three eggs
Allspice, beat very fine
Add sugar to your taste
A little salt
As much brandy and wine as you like

Put all ingredients together in a great pan. This 'mince-meat' mixture will keep good for months stored in a stone pot. When you bake your pies, lay a thin pastry crust over your tray, add the mincemeat mixture and cover with more short pastry.
Bake nicely in a hot oven.

⚜ FRUMENTY ⚜

Before the introduction of potatoes, frumenty was an old accompaniment to meat dishes. At one time it was the first food eaten on Christmas day. In Shropshire, every farmer put aside a sack of wheat which was distributed among the poor to make frumenty for the Christmas feast.

To make this dish the oldest recipe directs: 'Boil wheat until the grains burst, when cool, strain and boil again with broth of milk and yolk of eggs.'

CHRISTMAS CAKE.

When round the table we all sit
Papa gives each of us a bit,
And baby, too, must have a slice,
Because it is both sweet and nice.

THE CHRISTMAS CAKE

The present day traditional rich plum cake, with its coating of sugar has the beauty of its decorations limited only by the imagination of the maker of this Yuletide fare.

A rich Christmas cake requires lengthy beating, otherwise it is apt to be heavy.

CHRISTMAS CAKE RECIPE

1lb each of
butter and caster sugar
1lb each of
sultanas and currants, cleaned and dried
2lbs of flour
8 eggs
¾lb of mixed candied peel
½ an ounce of baking power
1 wineglass of brandy and a little milk

Beat the butter and sugar to a cream, and add the eggs one at a time, beating continuously. Sieve the flour and baking powder into a basin, and add the fruit, picked and cleaned, and the candied peel. Now add the flour and fruit, beating thoroughly and moistening with a little milk and the brandy, till the right consistency. Turn the mixture into a greased tin and bake in a moderate oven for about two hours, testing with a skewer, which should come out clean and dry if the cake is sufficiently baked. When quite cold, cover with icing and decorate.

❧ THE CHRISTMAS TABLE ❧

At the Christmas dinner table, place of honour *must* be given to the holly, with its abundance of red berries, placed in the centre of the table.

To take off the rather hard metallic look of the leaves, put mistletoe along with it. A poinsettia might be placed near the top of the table, that is, if the table is a large one.

At each guest's place put a small, narrow glass with a piece of maidenhair fern and mistletoe. Fold the table-napkins in the mitre shape, and put a tiny piece of holly with berries on each.

Menu cards might have a robin or other seasonable picture painted on them.

A MERRY CHRISTMAS

. . DINNER . .

Roast Turkey, Stuffed with Oysters
Cranberry Sauce
Mashed Potatoes   French Green Peas
White Plume Celery
English Plum Pudding, Brandy Dip
Assorted Cakes
Mince Pie
Coffee   Ice Cream
Cheese

⊰§ EGG NOGG AND MULLED WINE §⊱

Egg Nogg ~ Cold

Beat the yolks of two dozen eggs, together with one pound of finely pulverized sugar. Very slowly add one half gallon of brandy and one half pint of rum, stirring steadily. Pour in one quart of rich cream, then add the well-beaten egg whites. Add shaven ice. Store in a cool place.

Egg Nogg should always be served with grated nutmeg.

Egg Nogg ~ Hot

Whisk one egg and stir continuously while adding two teaspoons of sugar syrup, half a wineglass of rum and one wineglass of brandy. Fill the mixing bowl with hot milk, mix together and strain into a glass.

In mulling wine, care must be taken that the vessel is perfectly clean; otherwise, if it is greasy, or impregnated with any other flavour, it is apt to impart it, and spoil the wine.

Two Old-fashioned Recipes to Mull Wine ~ I

Into a clean stewpan pour one pint of water; add half an ounce of bruised ginger, cinnamon, cloves, nutmeg; cover up, and boil down to half pint of water; then strain clear, and add a quarter of a pound of sugar and one pint of claret.

To Mull Wine ~ II

Take a lemon and an orange, stick with cloves and roast by the open fire. Add to a pan one bottle of rich red wine, one pint of water, three ounces of sugar, one tablespoon of fruit liqueur, one teaspoon of ground ginger and one stick of cinnamon. Bring all ingredients to a gentle simmer. Add the lemon and orange and leave to brew on the fire for some time. When ready, ladle into glasses.

Into a skillet next you'll pour
A bottle of good wine, or more ...

Mulled Wine, with Eggs 1869

First, my dear madam, you must take
Nine eggs, which carefully you'll break
Into a bowl you'll drop the white,
The yolks into another by it.
Let Betsy beat the whites with a switch,
Till they appear quite froth'd and rich.
Another hand the yolks must beat
With sugar, which will make them sweet;
Three or four spoonfuls maybe'll do,
Though some, perhaps, would take but two
Into a skillet next you'll pour
A bottle of good wine, or more;
Put half a pint of water, too,
Or it may prove too strong for you:

And while the eggs by two are beating,
The wine and water may be heating;
But, when it comes to boiling heat,
The yolks and whites together beat.
With half a pint of water more –
Mixing them well – then gently pour
Into the skillet with the wine,
And stir it briskly all the time.
Then pour it off into a pitcher;
Grate nutmeg in to make it richer;
Then drink it hot, for he's a fool,
Who lets such precious liquor cool.

🎻 PARTIES AND ENTERTAINMENT 🎻

At **Christmas parties,** at which guests of all ages are to be found, it is sometimes a perplexing riddle to the hostess to know how to entertain them all.

Self-consciousness and shyness are often evident when the party enters the drawing-room, and this coating of ice, if not thawed quickly, will rapidly freeze into impenetrable restraint and gloom!

Musical items which may delight the older members of the company may only serve to render younger folk restless and dull, and dancing is not always possible in rooms of limited size. Moreover, there are still many young folk who are unable to set their feet nimbly to waltz or two-step, and would much prefer a romp to whirling round in time to a measure.

At such times a good game, quickly organised, is invaluable. The rules should be explained in so simple a manner that the youngest person can follow them, and everything necessary should be arranged beforehand to avoid awkward delays.

A rather good idea, which makes a pleasant change, is to adopt the following method when pairing off couples for festive supper: write out the name of a proverb on one slip of paper and the rest of it on another slip. Have as many slips as there are guests and let the ladies draw for the first parts and the gentlemen for the second parts of the proverbs. Much amusement is caused in the finding of partners and this plan will generally be found to be successful, especially at young people's parties.

Always include some guests who will be a
great help to you in entertaining with singing
carols and music.

When it comes to the games, let the revels be the simplest. 'Musical Chairs' and 'Hunt the Slipper' are great favourites with the children – any games which entail the crying of forfeits are also highly appreciated.

Other favourite games are 'Earth Air and Water' 'Family Coach' and 'Charades'.

Earth Air and Water

The players sit in a circle, and one throws a balloon to another, at the same time calling 'earth' (or 'air', or 'water'), and counting aloud up to ten. The one to whom he has directed the balloon must give the name of some animal that lives on the earth (or, if 'air' be called, of some bird; if 'water' of some fish) before the thrower has counted ten, paying a forfeit if he fails. That player sends the balloon on to some one else and so on. No animal, bird or fish may be repeated. Those not able to answer, sit out until there is a winner remaining.

Family Coach

This traditional game has been passed on in families down the years. The players must sit round the room and each chooses some part of the family coach: the wheel, the axle, the whip, the seat, Mrs Brown, her baby, the cat, &c.

One of the grown-ups then tells the tale of Mrs Brown's journey in the coach, and of the accidents that befell them; how one of the wheels came off, the axle broke, the baby cried, and so on, making it up as she goes along.

At the mention of each specific part, the member who has chosen that part must stand up and turn round. Should the words 'Family Coach' be mentioned, all the players must change seats. Should any fail to do this, or to answer his cue when his part is mentioned, he must pay a forfeit.

**Don't let there be any flagging in the enjoyment,
but a continual round of music, games,
dancing or conversation.**

Charades

The players divide into two groups. One group goes out of the room to choose a word with two or more syllables. Having chosen the word (which could be a book title), they decide to act a scene to illustrate the first syllable of the word. The more original the scene the better!

After this, they go out of the room again and decide how to bring in the other part of the word; acting another scene as they did the former. Having done this and used separately both syllables of the word, they have next to go through a scene in which they bring in the whole word. Then the other side is allowed three guesses in which to find the word.

If possible, the actors should dress up for their parts, as it causes much more fun, but in a small house, where there is no stock of spare clothes, this is often inconvenient, in which case it is best not to say anything about it.

TWELFTH NIGHT

In most places the greens and flowers are taken down after Twelfth Day.

"Down with the rosemary and so
Down with the baies and mistletoe
Down with the holly, ivie, all
Wherewith ye drest the Christmas hall;
That so the superstitious find
No one least branch there left behind
For look, how many leaves there be
Neglected there, maids, trust to me
So many goblins you shall see."

🔔 CHRISTMAS MISCELLANY 🔔

Stir Up Sunday

The last day of making Christmas cakes and pudding is the Sunday before Advent in late November called 'Stir up Sunday' from the Collect for the day 'Stir up we beseech thee ...'.

Wassail bowl

Named after the cry of 'Wass heil'. This was a drink made of old ale warmed, mixed with sugar, spices and beaten eggs, on top of which floated roasted apples, the whole being stirred with a sprig of rosemary. The Wassail bowl was indispensable to the old English Christmas.

Boxing Day

The day after Christmas Day is called Boxing Day and was traditionally when the Almsboxes were opened in churches for the poor and tradesmen broke into earthenware boxes which held the annual tips from their customers.

Pantomimes

Christmas pantomime was introduced in the early 18th century by Mr Rich who was a celebrated harlequin. The first pantomime in this country was in Drury Lane, London in 1702.

Victorian Turkeys

Many Victorian turkeys going to Christmas market were walked to London from Norfolk starting in August with their feet dipped in tar to prevent soreness. The turkeys were driven down the long march which lasted half a year, so that the birds left the farmer in the state of 'chickenhood' but arrived at the maturity of turkeyhood on the journey!

Before the 19th century, favourite meats for the Christmas feast were those which made a fine show on the table – peacock, swan and boar's head.

THE LEGEND OF CHRISTMAS ROSES

It is said that a shepherd girl followed her brothers to the inn and beheld the Wise Men presenting their gifts to the Babe. Her heart was filled with love for the Child and she wished to present something, but being poor she had nothing to give. Turning sadly away she wandered back to the woods and flung herself down.

The angel Gabriel appeared to her and asked the cause of her grief. Then the angel stretched out his hand and immediately the ground was covered with flowers peeping up through the snow. Full of joy the little maid gathered the precious Christmas roses, and returning to the stable she knelt and silently offered her gift. The sleeping Child awoke, and the flowers being touched by His tiny hand to this day carry a faint flush of gratitude upon their white petals.

May Your
Christmas be
a Happy One
And may the
New Year bring
You Contentment
and Prosperity
in overflowing
measure.

THE ETIQUETTE COLLECTION *Collect the set!*
ETIQUETTE FOR COFFEE LOVERS
Fresh coffee – the best welcome in the world!
Enjoy the story of coffee drinking,
coffee etiquette and recipes.

ETIQUETTE FOR CHOCOLATE LOVERS
Temptation through the years.
A special treat for all Chocolate Lovers.

THE ETIQUETTE OF NAMING THE BABY
'A good name keeps its lustre in the dark.'
Old English Proverb

THE ETIQUETTE OF AN ENGLISH TEA
How to serve a perfect English afternoon tea;
traditions, superstitions, recipes and how to read your
fortune in the tea-leaves afterwards.

THE ETIQUETTE OF ENGLISH PUDDINGS
Traditional recipes for good old-fashioned
puddings – together with etiquette notes
for serving.

ETIQUETTE FOR GENTLEMEN
*'If you have occasion to use your handkerchief
do so as noiselessly as possible.'*

ETIQUETTE FOR THE TRAVELLER
'There is nothing that a man can less afford to leave at home than his conscience or his good habits.'

ETIQUETTE FOR THE WELL-DRESSED MAN
A man is judged by his appearance.
'If you wear a morning coat your trousers will show more and must therefore be absolutely blameless.'

THE ETIQUETTE OF MOTORING
'Never take a sharp corner at full speed. A walking pace would be much better.'

THE ETIQUETTE OF DRESS
Learn how to be correctly dressed for all occasions.
A fine gift for anyone with an interest in fashion.

THE ETIQUETTE OF LOVE AND COURTSHIP
Essential advice for romantics.
Flirting, temptation, first impressions.

For your free catalogue, write to:

Copper Beech Publishing Ltd
P O Box 159 East Grinstead Sussex England RH19 4FS

www.copperbeechpublishing.co.uk